ABIDE:

LEARNING TO LIVE THE SPIRIT-FILLED LIFE THE WAY JESUS DID

R. Michael Coffey, D. Min.

ABIDE: LEARNING TO LIVE THE SPIRIT-FILLED LIFE THE WAY JESUS DID

Copyright © 2023 by R. Michael Coffey, D. Min.

All rights reserved. No part of this publication may be produced, stored in a retrieval system or transmitted in any form by any means, electronic, mechanical, photocopy, recording or otherwise, without the prior written permission of the author/publisher, except as provided by USA copyright law.

TABLE OF CONTENTS

Preface 4

Chapter One:
The Problem All Christians Face 5

Chapter Two:
The Difference Between Christ (the man) and Us 9

Chapter Three:
Understanding the Holy Spirit as a Person 14

Chapter Four:
The Apostle Paul Learns to Live the Spirit-Led Life 18

Chapter Five:
How Jesus Actually Lived the Perfect Life 27

Chapter Six:
The Truth Satan Doesn't Want You to Know 30

Chapter Seven:
Jesus Explains the Spirit-Filled Life 34

Chapter Eight:
The Secret of Living Like Christ 38

Chapter Nine:
Power Sourcing the Right Way 44

Chapter Ten:
Why Is the Church Confused About the Filling of the Spirit? 56

Chapter Eleven:
Promises of Christ to You 60

About the Author 63

PREFACE

Many Christians begin their new life in Christ with joy and excitement… but, over time, end up living defeated, ineffectual, and unsatisfying lives. What has changed from the days of the 1st century when Christians "filled [people] with wonder and amazement"? Is there a way for Christians not to lose their passion and enthusiasm, so that their impact on others is transformative?

In *Abide: Learning to Live the Spirit-filled Life the Way Jesus Did*, I discuss the way that Christ lived a perfect life as a man and His explanation of the way Christians can tap into the same power source He used. Through these 11 short chapters, Christians, regardless of where they are on their walk with God, can learn how Paul and the early disciples followed Jesus's guidance for living supernaturally.

This book explores the Scriptural truths about Christ's interaction with the Holy Spirit, revealing how the Spirit of Christ guides and empowers us to ultimate fulfillment and effectiveness, day by day, moment by moment—critically important truths for all of us.

Chapter One

The Challenge All Christians Face

The Christian life begins when you meet a person, Jesus Christ. This man, who lived for about 33 years, was God, living among His creations. He was truly the King, dressed as a pauper, who was revealed to be God and Lord when He was murdered but came back to life when He resurrected. Since that most important day in history (Easter morning), millions of people have encountered the risen Christ, usually by someone speaking about Him. When a person hears of the life, work, crucifixion, and resurrection of Christ, they are confronted with the most important truth they will encounter. It is a truth that requires action by them. They may choose to deny it, ignore it, procrastinate making a decision about its truthfulness... or they, like millions throughout history, may choose to believe that the God-man came to Earth to rescue them and anyone willing to believe the truth. Thus, those who believe that Christ, the innocent, died to pay a penalty for the sins of all humans, the guilty, decide to join Him in a new relationship that will never end.

Because He is God, proven by the resurrection, Jesus is able to do things people never imagined, like coming to live within them as His new dwelling place. As a result, this person, this new Christian, has both abundant and eternal life and can never lose it.

> "Whoever has the Son has life; whoever does not have the Son of God does not have life" (1 John 5:12);

> "...I have come that they may have life and have it to the full" (John 10:10).

This new life with Christ usually produces joy or at least relief in the minds and hearts of most people. *The Bible* begins to make sense when they read it; their fear of death and Hell is eliminated; many of them feel more peaceful than they have ever felt before, especially because God is attuned to each of us and loves us as His children. However, a new challenge emerges almost immediately.

Believing may turn into backsliding.

The new Christian may find that talking about Christ creates friction with some people, sometimes within their own family. They also find that although they want to obey the Scriptures, which finally make sense when they read them, they are unable to do the things they want to do or stop doing the things they don't want to continue doing. After an initial period of excitement and joy, new Christians find that thoughts, patterns, and habits re-emerge in their lives. Church services, *Bible* readings, Christian fellowship, and other events lose their excitement and may even begin to feel tedious or dull.

As a result, many new Christians begin pulling away from Christian activities and relationships, *Bible* reading, and prayer. The more these new Christians lose interest in spiritual things, the more they conform to their previous lifestyles and thought patterns. Some church traditions refer to this as "backsliding," which may become a habit. Occasionally, new Christians hear a speaker, or experience a Christian event and determine to "straighten up and get serious about God," only to backslide and lose interest again; renew again; and backslide again. It becomes a frustrating roller-coaster norm that many Christians eventually abandon, giving up all attempts to live as committed Christians.

Many of these same Christians may continue to attend and volunteer at their local church, so that they can "raise their children in the faith," or because they feel like it is the proper thing to do. They are sincere in their belief that Christ died for them and their sin, but they don't see how Christ has any effect on their day-to-day lives. They may fondly remember their initial excitement and joy of becoming a Christian, but those emotions now seem like feelings of a younger believer from long ago and far away. The promises of Christ to give an abundant life, living water, or rest from labors seem like religious sayings and nothing more. Such lofty promises are certainly not the reality experienced day by day.

Learning to live like Christ lived will help us fulfill what He promised.

This book hopes to aid all Christians in learning how to live the Christian life in the same way that Christ lived it when He walked upon the earth. He faced every temptation known to all people, but never sinned in over 33 years of life.

> "For we do not have a high priest who is unable to empathize with our weaknesses, but we have one who has been tempted in every way, just as we are—yet he did not sin" (Hebrews 4:15).

He dealt with people who were dull, stubborn, antagonistic, hateful, and even murderous. Throughout it all, He never failed to do the right and loving thing to all he met. Furthermore, He kept His relationship with God personal and vibrant. Living only 33 years in an obscure part of the world and doing public ministry for a little over 1,000 days, He changed the world forever AND was able to say that He accomplished everything that God wanted Him to accomplish.

> "I have brought You [God the Father] glory on earth by finishing the work You gave me to do" (John 17:4).

This book is also an attempt to explain how He did that and help us understand how to finally live the Christian life like Christ so that we can fulfill what He promised:

> "Very truly I tell you, whoever believes in me will do the works I have been doing, and they will do even greater things than these, because I am going to the Father" (John 14:12).

Chapter Two

The Difference Between Christ (the Man) and Us

Here is the major difference between Christ and us... when He walked the earth as a man, He recognized the cruciality of an inseparable, vibrant relationship with the Holy Spirit in His daily life. Moment by moment, He sought to be led, guided, taught, and empowered by the Holy Spirit.

In Luke's Gospel, we discover that Jesus was "full of the Holy Spirit," "led by the Spirit," (Luke 4:1–2), and came "in the power of the Spirit" (Luke 4:14).

Jesus began His public ministry by reading Isaiah 61:1–2 during a synagogue service, which emphasizes His relationship with the Holy Spirit:

> "The **Spirit of the Lord** is on me because he has anointed Me to proclaim good news to the poor. He has sent me to proclaim freedom for the prisoners and recovery of sight for the blind, to set the oppressed free, to proclaim the year of the Lord's favor."

He began by saying to them:

> "Today this Scripture is fulfilled in your hearing" (Luke 4:21).

Throughout the gospel accounts, Jesus is repeatedly said to be led by the Spirit, filled by the Spirit, and empowered by God. For example, Jesus was said to be "full of joy in the Holy Spirit" as He prayed to His heavenly Father in Luke 10:21.

Following Christ's example can be achieved by depending on the Holy Spirit.

Christ is a person's only hope of salvation because He was obedient to His Father's will and accomplished His perfect life and sacrificial death for us. ***However, it is equally true that Christ is the example of what is possible when a human lives his or her life in complete and total dependence upon the Spirit of God.***

How did that total dependence upon the Spirit of God affect Christ? He grew in wisdom, stature, and favor. He loved His enemies, forgiving those who did evil against Him while He humbly suffered injustice. He avoided all temptation while always telling the truth. Ultimately, He defeated Satan. How? By the power of the Holy Spirit.

When we read about Jesus in the gospel accounts, we see a man who experienced a range of emotions: exasperation, sadness and weeping, anger, longing for people to respond to God's outreach, intense pressure, joy, and optimism. Jesus, as the God-man, was fully man as well as fully God. As a man, the Scriptures teach that He learned obedience through the things He suffered (Hebrews 5:8) and grew in both physical size and wisdom (Luke 2:52). As a baby, growing into a man, He learned to dress Himself, perform work and chores, read, and study the Scriptures, and interact with others, including having theological discussions with religious leaders as a 12-year-old boy. Since Jesus was human, He needed to be filled, led, and empowered by the Holy Spirit daily. This empowerment by the Holy Spirit was evident as He questioned and answered the learned religious leaders in the Temple as a young boy. The Spirit's filling was again evident when He never sinned (John 8:46). It was Christ's close personal relationship with the Holy Spirit and His Father that empowered and equipped Him for ministry and holiness of life.

<u>Knowing the source of His power gave Jesus His abilities.</u>

How was Jesus able to do miracles as a man? Look at Peter's explanation to Cornelius in Acts 10:38:

> "... **God anointed Jesus of Nazareth with the Holy Spirit and power**, and how He went around doing good and healing all who were under the power of the devil, because God was with Him."

Later in His ministry, Jesus Himself confirmed the source of His power and abilities when He said:

> "... Very truly I tell you, **the Son can do nothing by Himself; He can do only what he sees his Father doing**, because whatever the Father does the Son also does" (John 5:19).

Christ modeled how to live a life of moment-by-moment reliance upon the Holy Spirit. It follows that to become more Christ-like in our daily lives, we need to do the things He did. Every moment of His life was connected to the Spirit. If we want to become more Christ-like, then we need to become more and more connected to, dependent upon, and empowered by the Spirit of God.

The public ministry of Jesus began with His baptism where the Holy Spirit was visibly present. At that baptism, John the Baptist said:

> "... I saw the Spirit come down from heaven as a dove and remain on Him. And I myself did not know Him, but the one who sent me to baptize with water told me, 'The man on whom you see the Spirit come down and remain is the one who will baptize with the Holy Spirit'" (John 1:32-33).

From this moment on, we always read about Jesus as the supremely wise, loving teacher and authoritative doer of miracles. Why? Because He never allowed Himself to be disconnected from the Holy Spirit for the rest of His brief life.

Obeying the Spirit's guidance allowed Jesus to overcome temptation.

You can see this connection in His first challenge after baptism – His temptation by Satan in the wilderness. The entire period of temptation showed His complete connectedness to the Holy Spirit, especially during the most difficult of circumstances.

> "Jesus, **full of the Holy Spirit**, left the Jordan and **was led by the Spirit into the wilderness**, where for forty days he was tempted by the devil" (Luke 4:1-2).

Christ was "**led**" by the Spirit into this wilderness testing period; He succeeded in overcoming the temptations of Satan because He was filled with the Spirit and obeyed the Spirit's guidance. This is why He could claim in His first speech in the synagogue following His temptation testing:

> "The Spirit of the Lord is on me, because He has anointed me" (Luke 4:18).

In fact, at that synagogue He could have chosen a previous passage from Isaiah to illustrate His source of wisdom, power, and holiness:

> "A shoot will come up from the stump of Jesse; from his roots a Branch will bear fruit. The **Spirit of the Lord** will rest on him—the **Spirit of wisdom** and of understanding, the **Spirit of counsel** and of might, the **Spirit of the knowledge** and fear of the Lord — and he will delight in the fear of the Lord" (Isaiah 11:1-3).

Throughout His ministry years, Christ attributed His miraculous powers to the Holy Spirit.

> "**But if it is by the Spirit of God** that I drive out demons, then the kingdom of God has come upon you" (Matt. 12:28).

Following Christ's example, we can also live Spirit-filled lives.

Some obvious questions should arise: "What would a Christian become or be like if he or she sought to be led, taught, and empowered by the Holy Spirit?" "How Christlike could Christians be if they followed His gameplan of being connected, led, and empowered by the Holy Spirit?" "How would my relationship to sin and with others be changed by living the Spirit-filled life like Christ did?" "What difference would the Spirit-prompted life make in my intimacy with God, my prayer life, my witness for Christ, my pursuit of holiness?"

I'll answer these questions in the following chapters, but first you need to know the good news is that **the Holy Spirit dwells inside every person when they become a Christian.** With Christ as our model, we can live an increasingly Spirit-filled life if we avail ourselves of the Spirit's presence and power, believe God's Word, and submit to the Spirit's leading as Jesus did. The Spirit-filled life is one in which our personal relationship with the Holy Spirit offers us the same power and Scripture-based wisdom that Jesus had when He became a man.

Chapter Three

Understanding the Holy Spirit as a Person

Have you ever wondered why the Holy Spirit seems to be the least understood Person in the Trinity? Some Christians don't even think of the Holy Spirit as a personality but consider Him more of an "it" or non-personal entity. This may be because, unlike the Father or the Son, the Holy Spirit does not speak from Himself or of Himself; instead, Christ said:

> "But when He, the Spirit of truth, comes, He will guide you into all the truth. **He will not speak on His own; He will speak only what He hears**, and He will tell you what is yet to come" (John 16:13).

Christ explains this further in the next verse saying the Spirit only shares what He has heard and been commissioned to share to ensure that Christ receives the glory:

> "He will glorify Me because it is from Me that He will receive what He will make known to you" (John 16:14).

There are instances in the Scripture where God the Father and the Son are speaking for themselves while using the personal pronoun "I," yet never in a rogue, uncoordinated manner. Jesus plainly stated:

> "For I did not speak on My own, but the Father who sent Me commanded Me to say all that I have spoken" (John 12:49).

The Godhead always operates in perfect coordination, communion, and cooperation with itself. However, this coordination and cooperation may make it more difficult for believers to grasp the personality of the Holy Spirit as easily as they perceive the Father's or the Son's personality. In fact, in the history of the Church, the personality of the Holy Spirit was not officially recognized and equated as divine with the Father and Son until the Nicene Creed in 325 A.D.

The Holy Spirit has distinguishing qualities.

Usually a "person" is defined as a being that has intellect, emotions, and will. The Scriptures clearly teach that the Holy Spirit has all three of these distinguishing qualities.

1. *Intellect* – The Holy Spirit does an in-depth search of the truths of God. He has a mind (Romans 8:27) and reveals the mind of God and the deep truths of God to people ("... these are the things God has revealed to us by his Spirit. The Spirit searches all things, even the deep things of God. For who knows a person's thoughts except their own spirit within them? In the same way, no one knows the thoughts of God except the Spirit of God" (1 Corinthians 2:10-11);

2. *Emotions* – Scripture reveals that the Holy Spirit has feelings - "And do not grieve the Holy Spirit of God, with whom you were sealed for the day of redemption" (Ephesians 4:30);

3. *Will* – The Holy Spirit decides and assigns spiritual gifts to Christians. "All these are the work of one and the same Spirit, and he distributes them to each one, just as he determines" (1 Corinthians 12:11).

There are many Scripture passages that reveal more about the Holy Spirit's personality:

- He reproves and convicts (John 16:8);
- He teaches, guides, and reveals (John 14:26; John 16:13-15);

- He has a voice and speaks in words (Galatians 4:6);
- He prays and intercedes for others (Romans 8:26);
- He leads (Galatians 5:18; Acts 8:29; Romans 8:14);
- He is sent to fulfill specific missions for God (John 15:26);
- He performs ministry: regenerating or making sinners born again (John 3:6); sealing (Ephesians 4:30); baptizing (1 Corinthians 12:13); filling (Ephesians 5:18);
- He fellowships with Christians (2 Corinthians 13:14); and
- He testifies (John 15:26; Romans 8:16).

Scripture also shows that since the Holy Spirit is a personality, He is affected by us:

- He can be vexed or annoyed by people (Isaiah 63:10);
- He can be grieved and resisted by people (Ephesians 4:30);
- People can quench or resist His leading (1 Thessalonians. 5:19);
- People can speak irreverently (blaspheme) about Him (Matthew. 12:31);
- People can lie to Him (Acts 5:3);
- He may be tested (Acts 5:9); and
- He can be disrespected and insulted by people (Hebrews 10:29).

Christ's relationship with the Holy Spirit was the secret to His success.

I share these proofs of the Holy Spirit's personhood because **His personal relationship** with Christ was the **critical component** to Christ's being able to live a sinless life **with unlimited access to God's power and wisdom.** Let the truth of that sentence seep deep into your mind and soul. If that was true for Christ, how can we ever hope to live a Christ-like life apart from the same Spirit upon whom Christ depended? Christ had a close, personal relationship with the Holy Spirit, and this relationship was the secret of His success in life and ministry. The wonderful news is that we CAN have a similar relationship with the Holy Spirit! The obvious question is "What difference would such a relationship make in our lives and service?"

Chapter Four

The Apostle Paul Learns to Live the Spirit-Led Life

When my children were little, we watched animated Disney movies like *Cinderella, Pinocchio,* or *Beauty and the Beast*. It was always exciting when magic happened, and a transformation occurred. Cinderella's rags were transformed into a beautiful ball gown; Pinocchio was changed from a wooden puppet to a real boy; the Beast was transformed from a hideous creature to a handsome prince. These metamorphoses happened instantly, with an outside power changing the Disney character.

<u>The power of the Holy Spirit is transforming.</u>

A much more true and powerful transformation occurs, however, when we become Christians, because the Holy Spirit immediately enters our lives.

> "Therefore, if anyone is in Christ, the new creation has come: The old has gone, the new is here!" (2 Corinthians 5:17).

What is gone; what is made new? All the Christian's sins (including future sins not yet committed) are forgiven. The person is changed from being unrighteous in God's sight to being clothed in the righteousness of Christ. God Himself, in the person of the Holy Spirit, chooses to dwell within you, His temple; you literally become the home of God! For the first time in your life, you are spiritually alive, experiencing a new relationship with God. He gives you a new identity—His adopted child—with spiritual gifts, new power, and authority on earth and in heaven to serve Him and His Church. Your citizenship is changed and transferred from a dying earth to the eternal kingdom of God. His transformation of you even gives you the mind of Christ if you choose to avail yourself of it.

It is a tragedy that many, if not most, Christians completely miss experiencing the changes God has already accomplished in their lives! It's as though paupers or prisoners are freed and elevated to royalty, but they choose to return to their impoverished state rather than embrace and live the new position imputed to them. But, when Christians truly grasp the possibilities and potential available to them through the person of the Holy Spirit, they immediately seek to improve their relationship with Him, which dynamically changes their lives.

The Apostle Paul transforms from religious anti-Christian zealot to a witness for God.

Let's turn to the Bible to see an example of a Christian grasping this truth and having his life dramatically changed as a result. The apostle Paul, before he became a Christian, was a religious zealot who tried to eradicate the emerging church in its infancy. Then, he met the risen Christ as he was traveling to Damascus to persecute Christians. After seeing the resurrected Christ, he became an outspoken witness, sharing with everyone how he had seen Christ resurrected and displayed with divine power. What is important to know is that although Paul became a Christian through that Damascus Road encounter and immediately tried to witness for God, **he did not learn how to live the Spirit-filled life for at least another decade**. Let's look at his journey as recorded in the pages of Scripture.

After his Damascus Road conversion:

> "Saul [Paul] spent several days with the disciples in Damascus. At once he began to preach in the synagogues that Jesus is the Son of God. All those who heard him were astonished and asked, 'Isn't he the man who raised havoc in Jerusalem among those who call on this name? And hasn't he come here to take them as prisoners to the chief priests?'" (Acts 9:19-21).

Because of the supernatural meeting with Christ, which Paul had experienced, he immediately began to preach, proclaim, or tell (ἐκήρυσσεν) others about it and his belief that the risen Christ was in fact God! But there is a time gap of possibly 3 years between verse 21 and verse 22, where Paul disappeared and isolated himself in Arabia. More about this period of his life in a moment.

Paul's ministry changed following 3 years in Arabia.

It wasn't important to Luke, the author of Acts, to note this 3-year time gap as he wrote the book of Acts, but it becomes important if one is to understand how Paul came to live the Christ-like life in the power of the Spirit. The narrative picks up Paul's life, after he returned from 3 years in Arabia in verse 22 noting:

> "Yet Saul [Paul] grew more and more powerful and baffled the Jews living in Damascus by proving that Jesus is the Messiah" (Acts 19:22).

This verse shows a different Paul than the Paul in verse 21. In verse 22, Paul is said to be "empowered" or "increasing in power" (ἐνεδυναμοῦτο) and that he was "proving" (συμβιβάζων) that Jesus was the Messiah, which is a change from the word for preaching or proclaiming that was used in verse 21. Why does changing a couple of words matter? Because we'll see Paul explaining in his own writings how he discovered the Christ-like way of living by depending upon the Holy Spirit.

What happened to Paul? He tells us in his letter to the Galatians about that early period in his life as a new Christian:

> "But when God, who set me apart from my mother's womb and called me by His grace, was pleased to reveal his Son in me so that I might preach Him among the Gentiles, my immediate response was not to consult any

human being. I did not go up to Jerusalem to see those who were apostles before I was, **but I went into Arabia** (for 3 years). **Later I returned to Damascus**" (Galatians 1:15-17).

The title "apostle" is often misused by some modern-day Christians and churches. An apostle is someone who saw the risen Lord AND received a commission from Him. This was a very small group of men in the 1st century, composed entirely of the original disciples of Jesus, and now Paul. Paul says that even though he was now an apostle, i.e., he had seen the risen Christ and was sent by Christ to witness to Gentiles, he did not go up to Jerusalem to meet with the other apostles of Jesus, but instead went away from Damascus to Arabia. While in Arabia for that 3-year period, he studied the Scriptures and spent time with the Holy Spirit, who led and taught him before he returned to Damascus. When Paul returned, he didn't just preach about Christ, but he "proved" his arguments in power and increasing strength… yet he still had much to learn about living the Spirit-filled life.

Paul faced persecution by the Jewish people.

Paul's proofs and arguments were presented in a more powerful fashion when he preached than when he was a new convert—so powerful that the Jewish people decided to kill him.

> "After many days had gone by, there was a conspiracy among the Jews to kill him, but Saul [Paul] learned of their plan. Day and night they kept a close watch on the city gates in order to kill him. But his followers took him by night and lowered him in a basket through an opening in the wall" (Acts 9:23-25).

God had commissioned him to be a witness to Gentiles, but his first ministry attempts since returning to Damascus resulted in an assassination plot and a hasty, quiet escape by darkness in a basket. By any standard, this was a humiliating beginning of a ministry. Paul began to learn one of the most fundamental truths of the Spirit-filled life: **God does not want to hurt your pride; He wants to KILL or COMPLETELY ELIMINATE it!**

<u>Barnabas introduced Paul to the other apostles.</u>

So, what's an apostle to do after such an ignoble exit? Paul finally goes to Jerusalem to meet with the other apostles of Christ.

> "When he came to Jerusalem, he tried to join the disciples, but they were all afraid of him, not believing that he really was a disciple. But Barnabas took him and brought him to the apostles. He told them how Saul on his journey had seen the Lord and that the Lord had spoken to him, and how in Damascus he had preached fearlessly in the name of Jesus. So, Saul stayed with them and moved about freely in Jerusalem, speaking boldly in the name of the Lord. He talked and debated with the Hellenistic Jews, but they tried to kill him" (Acts 9:27-29).

He is only welcomed because a trusted man named Barnabas introduced him to the apostles and the church in Jerusalem.

<u>God directed Paul to leave Jerusalem to witness to Gentiles.</u>

Paul immediately begins to use his powerful preaching and proving strategy, but it's déjà vu all over again with Hellenistic Jews attempting to assassinate him. Called by Christ to be a witness to the Gentiles, he must have been confused by the continual danger and opposition he encountered from Jewish people. No doubt distressed, Paul says that he went into the temple to pray and fell into a trance where Jesus spoke directly to him again:

> "When I returned to Jerusalem and was praying at the temple, I fell into a trance and saw the Lord speaking to me. 'Quick!' he said. 'Leave Jerusalem immediately, because the people here will not accept your testimony about me'" (Acts 22:17-18).

The Scriptural text doesn't give details, but it may indicate that Paul possibly struggled with the Lord about this command to leave Jerusalem immediately. Paul's response to God may have implied that his past record and sins as a persecutor of the church could be a powerful testimony to convert others, especially Jewish people. However, the Lord gives an emphatic command:

> "Then the Lord said to me, 'Go; I will send you far away to the Gentiles'" (Acts 22:21).

The church in Jerusalem agreed with this God-directed course of action:

> "When the believers learned of this, they took him down to Caesarea and sent him off to Tarsus (Paul's hometown)" (Acts 9:30).

Paul then disappears for 10 years. Ten years in his hometown is a long time to spend figuratively sleeping on your family's couch, especially when you have a direct commission from God!

The good news is that God is outside of space and time, so His way of preparing, training, and teaching us for effective ministry is not chained to a clock. If God let 10 years elapse in Paul's life in order to better prepare him for service, then it should be encouraging to all Christians that God knows how long you've been a Christian, and He's ready to use you, no matter how many years you've been a Christian WHEN you learn to live the Christ-like life in the power of the Spirit.

<u>Barnabas invited Paul to Antioch, where he launched his commission from Christ.</u>

Ten years after Paul returned to his hometown of Tarsus, his old friend Barnabas came looking for him again. Barnabas wanted Paul to accompany him to Antioch, where the church was experiencing a large numerical growth of new Gentile converts. Paul went with him, and for a year, he and Barnabas taught the Scriptures to the new believers of a rapidly growing church. Paul is finally fulfilling his commission from Christ, and the church grows, this time without an attempt on Paul's life. He and Barnabas are eventually dispatched by their church to carry an offering to help the Judean church during a famine crisis. This act of benevolence actually turns into a missionary launch of church planting that will continue for the rest of Paul's life. The missionary launch of Paul's ministry multiplied Christianity and the number of churches, impacting the world in a way that's never been equaled!

<u>God used Paul after he learned to use the power of the Holy Spirit.</u>

What made the difference? Paul had learned to lean on the Holy Spirit and the Scriptures for guidance and power RATHER than relying on himself, his strengths, gifts, and experience. God used Paul to write most of the New Testament, primarily in the form of letters to churches. In these letters he explains how he learned to live in a new way, experiencing the power, wisdom, and courage of Christ. Look at how he describes his moment-by-moment existence as a Spirit-filled follower of Christ:

> "I have been crucified with Christ and **I no longer live**, but **Christ lives in me**. The life I now live in the body, **I live by faith** in the Son of God, who loved me and gave himself for me" (Galatians 2:20);

"For it is we who are the circumcision, **we who serve God by his Spirit**, who boast in Christ Jesus, and **who put no confidence in the flesh**— though I myself have reasons for such confidence.

If someone else thinks they have reasons to put confidence in the flesh, I have more: circumcised on the eighth day, of the people of Israel, of the tribe of Benjamin, a Hebrew of Hebrews; in regard to the law, a Pharisee; as for zeal, persecuting the church; as for righteousness based on the law, faultless.

But whatever were gains to me I now consider loss for the sake of Christ. What is more, I consider **everything a loss** because of the surpassing worth of knowing Christ Jesus my Lord, for whose sake I have lost all things. **I consider them garbage, that I may gain Christ**" (Philippians 3:3-8);

"My conversation and my preaching were not with persuasive words of wisdom, **but with a demonstration of the Spirit and of power**, so that your faith would not be based on human wisdom but on the power of God" (1 Corinthians 2:4-5).

Paul sees a vivid contrast between someone trying to live the Christian life in their own strength, without the Spirit's power (which always fails), versus living their life by the power and guidance of the Holy Spirit:

"**But if you are led by the Spirit**, you are not under the law... the **fruit of the Spirit is love, joy, peace, patience, kindness, goodness, faithfulness, gentleness, and self-control**. Against such things there is no law. Now those who belong to Christ **have crucified the flesh with its passions and desires** [by the power of the Spirit, NOT their own strength nor effort]. **If we live by the Spirit**, let us also behave in accordance with the Spirit" (Galatians 5:18-25).

Paul had finally learned what God truly wants for all believers. God wants Christians, indwelled by the Holy Spirit, to learn to trust the Spirit for guidance and to avail themselves of the same power Christ used to live His life. Contrary to the way many Christians live their entire lives, He wants us to stop trying to live the Christian life with our own strength, talents, resources, and skills. Instead, He wants us to understand and learn to live a radically effective life, which God supplies through the Holy Spirit who indwells every Christian.

There is a Who's Who list of Biblical evidence of the power of a Spirit-filled life.

When we learn to live the Spirit-filled life, we avail ourselves of the power, wisdom, and resources of Almighty God living in each of us. This Spirit is the Person who turned a proud, overconfident Paul into the author of most of the New Testament and the catalyst founder of the Christian church. It is the same Spirit that turned a cowardly Peter into a bold preacher, who preached for 1 minute on Pentecost morning, and established the Church of Christ with 3,000 new converts. It is the same Spirit who guided a humble man like Barnabas to courageously befriend Paul, the former persecutor of the church, and established him in ministry after his Damascus Road experience. The list of those who learned to rely on the Spirit's wisdom, guidance, and power lists as a Who's Who throughout history of the Church. Will you be the next one to learn the secret of the Christ-like life?

Chapter Five

How Jesus Actually Lived the Perfect Life

Jesus lived a life entirely dependent upon the Holy Spirit. Even before His birth, the Holy Spirit was active in Christ's life and the lives of others in the nativity story. His mother was impregnated by the power of the Holy Spirit. The nativity account notes that:

> "Now the birth of Jesus the Messiah was as follows: when His mother Mary had been betrothed to Joseph, before they came together, she was found to be pregnant **by the Holy Spirit**" (Matthew 1:18).

This validated what the archangel Gabriel had told Mary when he appeared to her:

> "The angel answered and said to her, "**The Holy Spirit will come upon you, and the power of the Most High will overshadow you**; for that reason also the Holy Child will be called the Son of God" (Luke 1:35).

When a pregnant Mary visited her relative Elizabeth, the Scriptures note:

> "When Elizabeth heard Mary's greeting, the baby leaped in her womb, **and Elizabeth was filled with the Holy Spirit**" (Luke 1:41).

Elizabeth's husband Zachariah also encountered the Holy Spirit and when his son John the Baptist was born, Zachariah was released from his temporary muteness and:

> "...**Zechariah was filled with the Holy Spirit** and prophesied, saying: Blessed *be* the Lord God of Israel, For He has visited *us* and accomplished redemption for His people" (Luke 1: 67-68).

Simeon is led by the Holy Spirit at the presentation of Jesus at the temple.

When Jesus was presented as an infant at the Jerusalem temple, the Holy Spirit moved and guided an old man named Simeon to meet Christ's family and then spoke through him to declare Jesus to be the Messiah:

> "And there was a man in Jerusalem whose name was Simeon; and this man was righteous and devout, looking forward to the consolation of Israel; **and the Holy Spirit was upon him**. And **it had been revealed to him by the Holy Spirit** that he would not see death before he had seen the Lord's Christ. And **he came by the Spirit** into the temple; and when the parents brought in the child Jesus, to carry out for Him the custom of the Law, then he took Him in his arms, and blessed God, and said,
>
>> "Now, Lord, You are letting Your bond-servant depart in peace, According to Your word; For my eyes have seen Your salvation, Which You have prepared in the presence of all the peoples: A light for revelation for the Gentiles, And the glory of Your people Israel" (Luke 2:25-32).

The Holy Spirit had influence in the life of Jesus.

As noted earlier, the Spirit was critical to the success of Jesus as He began His public ministry. At his baptism, the Spirit descended from heaven upon Him in the form of a dove; the Spirit led him into the wilderness to struggle against the Devil's temptations for 40 days; His first statement after the wilderness temptation was in a synagogue where He claimed the Spirit of the Lord was upon Him, saying He fulfilled the prophecy found in Isaiah 61:1-11.

Then for 3 years of public ministry, the gospel accounts are filled with stories of Jesus performing astonishing miracles of healing diseases, controlling nature, and casting out demons – ALL while noting that Jesus was continually filled by the Spirit; activated the power of the Spirit; and was dependent upon the power of the Spirit for His ability to speak authoritatively, do good, and help people. Time and time again, the various gospel accounts note the dependency of Christ upon the Holy Spirit for everything He did in life:

"This happened so that what was spoken through Isaiah the prophet would be fulfilled:

> 'Behold, My Servant whom I have chosen; My Beloved **in whom My soul delights; I will put My Spirit upon Him**, And He will proclaim justice to the Gentiles. He will not quarrel, nor cry out;
>
> Nor will anyone hear His voice in the streets. A bent reed He will not break *off*, And a dimly burning He will not extinguish, Until He leads justice to victory. And in His name the Gentiles will hope'" (Matthew 12:17-21).

How did Christ live, day by day, moment by moment, filled with the Holy Spirit? The answer is found during His Last Supper with His disciples, prior to His arrest and crucifixion. However, before we study Christ's teaching at His Last Supper, we will first look at God's plan for all Christians from eternity past.

Chapter Six

The Truth Satan Doesn't Want You to Know

As was established earlier in Chapter 2, Jesus was able to live a perfect life and accomplish everything His Father wanted Him to do, because He relied upon and was filled with the Holy Spirit every moment of His earthly life. Christians diminish His obedience when they say, "Oh, it was easier for Jesus to obey and live sinlessly because He was God." Nothing could be further from the truth! When Christ lived among people, He chose to lay aside what was rightfully His, as part of the Trinity, choosing to live as a man.

Jesus chose to live with the limitations of a human.

> "Have this attitude in yourselves which was also in Christ Jesus, who, as He already existed in the form of God, did not consider equality with God something to be grasped, but emptied Himself by taking the form of a bondservant and being born in the likeness of men" (Philippians 2:5-7).

Jesus, a perfect man, chose to live with all the limitations of a human so that He could die as a substitute and pay the sin penalty owed by all the imperfect humans who have ever lived. The fact that He accomplished such a monumental task shows us how differently we could live if we availed ourselves of the same power source that filled Him and that He continuously depended on – the Holy Spirit.

Many will say that it is impossible to live the Christian life like Christ did. That's true simply because we love sin and rebellion... not because the Holy Spirit's power is diminished in any way. He is just as willing to lead, guide, empower, and work wonders through us as He was to work through Jesus Christ. We are the ones who break the circuit of power to Him.

The impact of the Holy Spirit is real.

We also see that supernatural change in the lives of the disciples. After His resurrection, Jesus appeared to them and told them to wait until they had received the Holy Spirit (Acts 1:8), and then they would be His witnesses. As soon as the Holy Spirit filled them on Pentecost morning, they began immediately to do the things people had only seen Jesus doing--preaching and teaching with great authority, healing the sick, raising the dead, and casting out demons.

The Holy Spirit established His Church through which Christ currently works in the world.

At this point, many Christians will stop reading to protest, "Yes, but God's Spirit doesn't work like that any longer. He did the miraculous through the disciples to authenticate them as Christ's representatives and to authenticate God's new entity, called 'the Church' or 'the Body of Christ.'" I would agree with that statement… to a point. I do believe that the Spirit did miraculous signs and wonders through the original disciples to establish them as Christ's witnesses and representatives on Earth after He left Earth and ascended to Heaven. I also believe the Holy Spirit did miracles to establish His Church as the agency through which Christ currently works in the world. This new agency, His Church, differs from Israel, the former agency through which He interacted with the world for centuries. In His Church, there are no longer Jews or Gentiles, males or females, slaves or free people… but all are simply disciples or followers of Christ, now known as Christians.

The Holy Spirit is still at work in miraculous ways, while our powerlessness is proof of unbelief and sin.

HOWEVER, IT IS IMPORTANT TO REALIZE that the Holy Spirit can STILL do ANY miracle or miraculous sign He wishes to do! He can do it through any believer, at any time, in any location IF He (the Holy Spirit) chooses to do it in obedience to Christ or the Father's will so that Christ is glorified (John 16:14). Why else would Christians be commanded to seek anointment with oil and prayer for healing by elders of their church if God was unwilling to still do miracles (James 5:14-15)? The powerlessness of our Christian lives, experience, and ministries is proof of our unbelief and sin rather than a proof that the Holy Spirit no longer works the miraculous in the present age!

Satan is constantly at work undermining the Christian way of life.

Once you understand the truth, it makes sense WHY this campaign of disinformation is one of Satan's main strategies to battle against the Lord. Satan already lost a critical battle with each Christian's conversion. Each Christian is forgiven and guaranteed eternal life with Christ. Since that battle is already lost by Satan, then the 2nd most important fight is to ensure that Christians NEVER understand the power available for them to live like Christ, day by day, moment by moment through the power of the Holy Spirit. If Satan can discourage, confuse, and defeat Christians through a disinformation campaign, then he effectively reduces the Church of Christ to a hollow army – weak, ineffective, sinful, and inconsequential to the spiritual battle raging between Satan and God. Satan would like nothing better, after you are freely forgiven for your sins, than to convince you that you must "try harder" to obey the Scriptures and "please God" by your own efforts. It is an impossible and futile way of living the Christian life... and Christians have been failing at it since the start of the Church.

<u>Satan does not have the final word...Christ does through the Holy Spirit.</u>

How do we stop the futility and begin to live in the power of Christ through the Holy Spirit? The answer is found in Christ's Last Supper discourse with His disciples.

Chapter Seven

Jesus Explains the Spirit-Filled Life

At His Last Supper with His disciples before His arrest and death, Jesus shocked His disciples by telling them hard truths, one after another. He told them that He was leaving them (John 13:33) after being betrayed by one of the disciples (13:21), that Peter would deny him three times before the morning (John 13:38), that Satan would attack all of them (Luke 22:31-32), and that they would all run away when danger arose (Matthew 26:31). He takes this last teaching opportunity to: (1) comfort them and promise that He will return for them; (2) introduce the personhood of the Holy Spirit and His role in the lives of the disciples and all future believers; and (3) explain how He had lived in perfect obedience and power through the Holy Spirit.

Christ explains the unity and interdependency of the Trinity.

Christ explains to His disciples that the Godhead works in perfect unity and in perfect subjection. All three members of the Trinity are equally God, but they choose to work with the Father commanding and sending the Son or Spirit: the Son commanding or sending the Spirit, and the Spirit always acting in the world so that Christ receives the glory. Jesus re-explains this when Phillip asks Him to show the disciples the Father (thinking they would see God the Father like Moses or Isaiah had seen Him). Jesus answers Phillip's request by teaching about the unity and interdependency of the Trinity:

> "Philip said to Him, "Lord, show us the Father, and it is enough for us." Jesus said to him, "Have I been with you for so long a time, and yet you have not come to know Me, Philip? The one who has seen Me has seen the Father; how can you say, 'Show us the Father'? **Do you**

not believe that I am in the Father, and the Father is in Me? The words that I say to you I do not speak on My own, but the Father, as He remains in Me, does His works. Believe Me that I am in the Father and the Father is in Me; otherwise believe because of the works themselves"** (John 14: 8-11).

<u>Jesus promises to ask His Father for another Helper like Himself after He leaves.</u>

This explanation of the unity and interdependency of the Trinity should help the disciples grasp what He plans to teach them about His reliance upon the Holy Spirit for the wisdom and power they have seen Him exhibit for the past 3 years. He tells them He'll ask His Father to give them another (i.e., same kind) of "Helper" or "Counselor" as Himself, who will live inside of them after He leaves, and that the Holy Spirit will help them to understand how this relationship with the Spirit will be the key to their success, just as it was the key to His success:

> "I will ask the Father, and He will give you **another Helper**, so that He may be with you forever; the Helper is the Spirit of truth, whom the world cannot receive, because it does not see Him or know Him; but you know Him because He remains with you and **will be in you**" (John 14: 16-17).

> "I will not leave you as orphans; I am coming to you. After a little while, the world no longer is going to see Me, but you are going to see Me; because I live, you also will live. **On that day you will know that I am in My Father, and you are in Me, and I in you.** The one who has My commandments and keeps them is the one who loves Me; and the one who loves Me will be loved by My Father, and I will love him and will reveal Myself to him" (John 14:18-21).

Christ lived His life constantly filled with the Holy Spirit.

Christ continues to explain how He lived His life in the next verses by showing His constant connectedness with His Father and the Holy Spirit and reminding the apostles that, as a man, He was dependent upon His Father and the Spirit to know what to say or do for the past 3 years:

> Jesus answered and said to him, "If anyone loves Me, he will follow My word; and My Father will love him, and **We will come to him and make *Our* dwelling with him**. The one who does not love Me does not follow My words; and **the word which you hear is not Mine, but the Father's, who sent Me**" (John 14:23-24).

THIS illustrates how Christ lived His Spirit-filled life! He was constantly filled with the Spirit (which is NOW a possibility for all believers since Christ has sent the Spirit to reside in each Christian). He only spoke what His Father, through the Spirit told Him to speak, or do obediently what the Father, through the Spirit, told Him to do.

Christians can also live a Spirit-filled life with the help of the Scriptures.

Christians also have this possibility today BECAUSE we have His Spirit living within us. Furthermore, we have a completed Scripture to read and hear directly from Christ as we live our day-to-day lives! He is willing to speak to us through the Scriptures at any time, so we can obey what He tells us to do! The Holy Spirit, who inspired the Scriptures to be written, is willing to bring Scripture to our mind as needed to live effectively for Christ!

Christians who want to live a Christlike life, full of wisdom and power, need to spend time daily in God's Word so they can better hear what Christ and the Spirit want them to do in obedience. It's cultivating a relationship, listening to the voice of Christ in the

Scriptures as you read them, and listening to the voice of the Spirit inside you as you live moment by moment. You won't do this perfectly at first, but it IS possible to grow more Christlike every day by beginning this lifestyle, depending upon the Spirit to lead, guide, teach, and empower you. **Time, submission, and obedience to the Spirit and the Word WILL produce the Christlike character all Christians should want!**

Christ, who was the Master Teacher, will next give His disciples and us an illustration of how He lived in perfect union with the Father and the Spirit and how it enabled Him to "bear fruit" and do everything His Father wanted Him to accomplish.

I believe you will be greatly encouraged as you read on to see how He explains the process.

Chapter Eight

The Secret of Living Like Christ

Final words have great importance and often a lasting impact. Deathbed statements carry great weight, because the time for talk is ending, and the topic being discussed is of great importance for the speaker to communicate to listeners. That is exactly what occurred in Jesus's Upper Room discourse to His disciples. In John 15, Jesus explains the way for Christians to live a Spirit-filled life, moment by moment, every day.

Jesus is the true vine and bears much fruit; He has a relationship with God and is obedient to Him.

The Israeli people (including Christ's disciples) had been taught all their lives that Israel was "the vine" for which God the Father, as the vinedresser, loved and cared. This was based on several Old Testament passages which clearly taught this (Psalm 80:8; Isaiah 5:1-7; Jeremiah 2:21; 6:9; Ezekiel 15; 17:5-10; 19:10-14; Hosea 10:1; 14:8). God the Father had longed for Israel to produce fruit for Him, but the vine (Israel) degenerated instead of bearing fruit. Here is what Jesus has said:

"I am the true vine, and My Father is the vinedresser" (John 15:1).

Jesus is shocking His disciples by telling them that now HE, and not Israel, is the true vine for which the Father (the gardener) loves, protects, and tends. Unlike the nation of Israel, Christ sought a relationship with God the Father AND sought to obey and do everything the Father wanted. **RELATIONSHIP AND SUBMISSIVE OBEDIENCE – these are core elements of the Spirit-filled life!** Christ did both and therefore accomplished everything the Father wanted Him to accomplish, i.e., HE BORE much fruit!

Bearing fruit means having a relationship with Christ, the vine.

Christ makes a simple distinction about all Christians – some seem to be "in Me" but bear no fruit, while others "in Me" DO bear fruit. Bearing fruit is the proof of your union or relationship with Christ. God the Father tends and prunes those who are in union or relationship with Christ so they can produce more fruit. If the Father does not see any fruit, then the branch is removed:

> "Every branch in Me that does not bear fruit, He takes away; and every branch that bears fruit, He prunes it so that it may bear more fruit" (John 15:2).

Biblical scholars disagree whether the non-fruit-bearing branches are non-Christians who profess that they are believers, or whether the phrase means worldly, immature, and peripheral Christians who do not pursue relationship with Christ or obedience to His Word. I believe that branches that bear no fruit, prove that they do NOT have a union or relationship with the vine (Christ).

There are nine characteristics of the fruit of the Spirit that were modeled by Christ model in ministry.

What does Christ mean by "fruit" and the phrase," bear fruit"? I believe "bear fruit" means Christians are in a growing, deepening relationship with Christ, so that they become more like Him day by day and reflect Him to others. *The Bible* teaches:

> "But the fruit of the Spirit is love, joy, peace, patience, kindness, goodness, faithfulness, gentleness, self-control" (Galatians 5:22-23).

This verse describes the Spirit-filled life that Christ lived for 30+ years. These are the characteristics that sinners found so attractive and irresistible they followed Christ, sometimes in throngs, and longed to listen to Him. The fruit God wants is to see

Christians displaying these characteristics of Christ through their daily lives. These characteristics should attract others to Christ because they see Christ through you and me. Bearing fruit is both living as a new creation to intrigue and attract people and then witnessing about Christ's saving grace to those people so they may become a new creation as well. This was Christ's model in ministry.

<u>Christians cannot bear fruit unless they have a close relationship with Christ.</u>

Christ continues to explain the Spirit-filled life:

> "You are already clean because of the Word which I have spoken to you (the truth Christ taught). Remain in Me, and I in you. Just as the branch cannot bear fruit of itself but must remain in the vine, so neither can you unless you remain in Me. I am the vine, you are the branches; the one who remains in Me, and I in him bears much fruit, for apart from Me you can do nothing" (John 15:3-5)

The vine and branches contain the same life, the same substance or essence. The vine is the source that pumps life to the branch, where the sole purpose of the branch is to produce the fruit that flows from the vine. The vine exists to feed and grow the branches. The branches exist solely to bear the fruit that comes from the vine.

> "If anyone does not remain in Me, he is thrown away like a branch and dries up; and they gather them and throw them into the fire, and they are burned" (John 15:6).

This isn't a reference to eternal punishment, but simply an acknowledgment that in any orchard, a branch that doesn't bear fruit is removed and eliminated, because it has no other purpose or usefulness. It only exists to bear fruit.

"If you remain in Me, and My words remain in you, ask whatever you wish, and it will be done for you. My Father is glorified by this, that you bear much fruit, and so prove to be My disciples. Just as the Father has loved Me, I also have loved you; remain in My love. If you keep My commandments, you will remain in My love; just as I have kept My Father's commandments and remain in His love. These things I have spoken to you so that My joy may be in you, and that your joy may be made full" (John 15:7-11).

Christ was always connected to God the Father by the Holy Spirit and obeyed the Scriptures.

Christ explains the interconnectedness of the Spirit-filled life – staying in a love relationship with Him; letting His words have authority and influence in our day-to-day living. He explains that He kept the love relationship with His Father, obeying the Scriptures ("my Father's commandments") with the result of remaining in His Father's love. Christ was always connected to His Father by the Holy Spirit (abiding); so, He always knew what His Father wanted done ("just as I have kept My Father's commandments"); and furthermore, He was able to "remain in His [Father's] love."

Living like Christ in the power of the Holy Spirit is exciting! The secret is revealed by:

- **Submissive abiding, connecting, or remaining in Christ, who is the True Vine;**
- **Obeying the Scriptures as the Spirit brings them to light when you face daily trials and temptations; and**
- **Exhibiting the life of Christ, also known as the fruit of the Spirit, more and more each day when you**

submit, abide, or remain in Him, and obey His Word.

Paul submitted and abided in Christ.

The phrase John the Baptist used with his disciples about Christ wasn't describing the Spirit-filled life, BUT it could have! John told his disciples, "**He must increase, but I must decrease**" (John 3:30). That is an excellent description of submitting and abiding in Christ, so the life of Christ can be seen in you where previously people could only see you.

The Apostle Paul, once he understood the Spirit-filled life and began to live it, could say:

> "I have been crucified with Christ; and **it is no longer I who live, but Christ lives in me**; and **the life which I now live in the flesh I live by faith** in the Son of God, who loved me and gave Himself up for me" (Galatians 2:20); or

> "**For to me to live is Christ**, and to die is gain" (Philippians 1:21); or

> "But I say, **walk by the Spirit, and you will not gratify the desires of the flesh**" (Galatians 5:16).

Jesus was the one and only perfect example of living the Christian life.

Once again, only ONE person has ever successfully and completely lived the Christian life – Jesus!

Only one person is capable of living it - Jesus! However, He did not want us to be discouraged about not being able to live the perfect life, because we are imperfect human beings. But rather, He gives us the choice of abiding or remaining in Him, the True Vine, so that His life can flow into each of us, the branch. When the character traits of Christ begin to develop in my day-to-day life, then I am bearing fruit. Christ says His Father wants fruit, more fruit, and much fruit. His clear teaching is:

> "Remain in Me, and I in you. Just as the branch cannot bear fruit of itself but must remain in the vine, so neither can you unless you remain in Me" (John 15:4).

While bearing fruit as we submit and abide in Christ, we must also learn how to benefit from the great source of power available within every one of us through the Holy Spirit. And believe it nor not, there is a wrong way and a right way.

Chapter Nine

Power Sourcing the Right Way

If you are seeking to live by your own power or abilities instead of tapping into the power of the Holy Spirit residing in you to help you, then you are a Christian who doesn't understand power sourcing. The true source of power for the Christian to live a Christ-like life can be illustrated by a man purchasing an electric vehicle. When you became a Christian, the initial power, excitement, emotion, and other "charges" you may have felt, may have been a feeling like the one you felt in an electric vehicle effortlessly gliding along the road when you test drove it at the dealership. Your initial excitement about being forgiven, reading the Bible, and attending church was new and continues for a while, but eventually, that enthusiasm, like an electric car, slows and finally stalls.

Let's take the metaphor a little further. Many new electric car owners, finding that their vehicle no longer works, would be embarrassed to not be seen with the vehicle they've told family, or friends that they've bought and to which they've made a commitment. So, they begin to push the car to work (maybe arriving early so others won't see them pushing). They still admire the vehicle, its attractive design, upholstery, custom speaker system, and other parts of the design and remember with waning joy the feeling they had when it first became a part of their life. However, if truth be told, they begin to resent having to push it anywhere they want to go. They may ask questions or read to see if others have had a similar disappointing experience after the initial joy and excitement of purchasing and driving the vehicle. They find that many do, and some places even have instructional seminars about pushing vehicles without injury, or mapping routes that involve fewer hills.

Like the fictitious vehicle owner, occasionally, the Christian may encounter and be intrigued by other Christians talking about "recharging" or quickly "boosting" their "spiritual vehicle" as power drains. They find those articles that stir hopefulness within them to be confusing or lacking in explanation of how to get this "charge" or "boost."

This silly illustration is exactly how much (if not most) of Christianity is being lived today. We spend hours at churches teaching people how to use all their human resources to "keep trying harder to work for God!" Sadly, many churches are instructing Christians how to mobilize their own energy, will, talents, and strengths to do something that is impossible for them to do. Let's restate a key point from earlier in this book: **only one person has ever lived the perfect Christian life – only that person, Jesus, will ever be able to live it.**

Christians are often unaware of the unlimited power source available to them.

Returning to the metaphor, if we want to help the man pushing the electric vehicle, we need to help him push his car to a battery charger at the closest corner. Then we explain how to hook up his vehicle for recharging. While it recharges, we point out that an unlimited power source is available throughout the city in the form of free chargers. The man is amazed when we explain that the same power technology is also at his home; it turns out he was confused and didn't understand the purpose of the charging unit that came with the car when it was installed in his garage. Slowly, finally, the man begins to understand that his responsibility is to tap into the endless energy available to him. Infinite access to a power recharger!... The grand designer of his electric vehicle knew the owner would have the problem of power loss. **What the designer never anticipated was that the vehicle owner would try to solve this problem with his own,**

limited, failing strength and resources. Unlike so many Christians who never learn about the Christ-filled life, this Christian has now learned that the vehicle, with repeated charging, is equal to whatever demands will be faced when driven.

God supplies an unlimited power source—Jesus, who resides in us as the Holy Spirit.

Now **that** is what the Christ-filled (i.e., the Spirit-filled life) is all about. God knew that we Christians are not able to meet the demands that life makes upon us on our own, so he supplied an unlimited power source--the person of Jesus, residing in each of us as the Holy Spirit. The Spirit is more than capable of handling any event, circumstance, problem, or person. Our part is to learn to switch to the **correct power source** so we can begin to experience the restfulness of activity in the strength of the Spirit. To be connected to the Spirit and His power, we need to learn to choose and make three key choices.

There are three commands found in Scripture that are necessary to be filled with the Holy Spirit.

What are the "choices" we need to make to live the Spirit-filled life? Scripture only lists three commands for believers to follow:

"Do not quench the Spirit" (1 Thessalonians 5:19);

"Do not grieve the Holy Spirit of God, by whom you were sealed for the day of redemption" (Ephesians 4:30); and

"But I say, walk by the Spirit, and you will not carry out the desire of the flesh" (Galatians 5:16).

Each one is related to the other, which I will now explain with support from the Scriptures.

DO NOT QUENCH THE SPIRIT

The command, "Do not quench the Spirit" in 1 Thessalonians 5:19, uses a fire motif to illustrate the Spirit's active work in the believer's life. Quenching the Spirit's leading, guidance, or work is just like snuffing a fire. A believer may quench, snuff, or stifle the Spirit's role in their life by a simple "No" or unwillingness to let the Spirit lead. Rebellion has existed since Satan's original act of defiance and Adam's and Eve's willful disobedience. "I will!" always stands in rebellious contrast to Jesus's submissive "... yet not My will, but Yours be done" (Luke 22:42). Christ's reply shows a man filled with the Holy Spirit. Resisting the leading of God and saying "I will!" is a person's first step in quenching the Holy Spirit.

Christians need to understand the expectation to continually submit to God.

Sometime after a person becomes a Christian, the Holy Spirit directs that person to passages such as:

> "No one can serve two masters; for either he will hate the one and love the other, or he will be devoted to one and despise the other. You cannot serve God and wealth" (Matthew 6:24)

This is to help the new believer begin to understand the expectation to continually submit to God. Romans 6:13 puts that expectation plainly when it says every believer either yields to God or yields to sin. A passage often used by the Holy Spirit to illustrate this growing yielding to God in a believer's life is:

> "Therefore, I urge you, brothers *and sisters*, by the mercies of God, to present your bodies as a living and holy sacrifice, acceptable to God, *which is* your spiritual service of worship. And do not be conformed to this world, but be transformed by the renewing of your mind, so that you may prove what the will of God is,

that which is good and acceptable and perfect" (Romans 12:1,2).

Scriptures guide us to choose to be a living sacrifice for God.

The Greek verb "to yield" used in both Romans 6:13 and Romans 12:1-2 is an "aorist" tense, which means a once-and-for-all decision to yield to God. In the Old Testament, if a person wanted to remain as a bondservant to the master and house where he formerly served as a slave, he would request the master to split his ear lobe with an awl. This marked him as a bondservant who willingly (once and for all) chose to be a servant to the master. It was a choice the person made, but it had a lasting effect upon his life. This is the point of Romans 12:1-2, where Christians are urged to "present themselves" willingly by figuratively climbing upon an altar "as a living and holy sacrifice" for God.

A sacrifice in the Old Testament was a one-time event (you couldn't keep sacrificing the same animal or offering over and over). While it's true that we, as living sacrifices, may choose to "quench the Spirit" by climbing off the altar, it is actually the Spirit guiding us, the believers, with these Scripture passages toward having a heart and volitional attitude of choosing to be a "living sacrifice" for God. The initial act of saying, "I want to be a living sacrifice for You Lord" is a once-and-for-all decision to give your life to the Lord for His use. A living sacrifice doesn't say how it is willing to be sacrificed... he or she simply submits. The bondservant with the split earlobe, or a living sacrifice – both choose to make that permanent, once-and-for-all decision.

When Christians make the decision to offer themselves to the Lord as living sacrifices, the Romans 12:1-2 passage says that outward conformity to the world begins to be swapped with a transformed mind and godly actions that prove "what the will of God is, that which is good and acceptable and perfect."

It is important to understand the concept of "yieldedness."

Yieldedness is a key component of not quenching the Spirit. This command is a present tense command in the original Greek text, which means it is to be a continual action and experience, started by an initial act of yieldedness. The Holy Spirit, whom Christ promised to send to lead and guide believers, begins to immediately highlight Scriptures to the new believer from which to learn and grow in maturity. Submitting to the Word of God is one of the first and never-ending yielding every believer chooses. Refusal to do so, as the Spirit brings a passage to light, will quench the Spirit and make the filling of the Spirit an impossibility.

Christians need to learn to be guided by the Spirit and His use of the Word to communicate His will.

Equally true, since the Scriptures do not explicitly address every decision a Christian will have to make throughout their life, the believer must learn to be guided by the Spirit and the Spirit's use of the Word of God to navigate some decisions in life. Early in his Christian life, Paul wanted to travel to Asia and preach the Gospel, but the Spirit denied him permission; yet later the same Spirit instructed Paul to go to that same region and preach. Being filled with the Spirit involves yielding in obedience to the Spirit's guidance as He uses Scripture to communicate His will. Thus, it is essential for the Christian to yield his or her desires for the preference of the Spirit.

This continual yieldedness and obedience to the guidance of the Spirit and the Scriptures then enables the Christian to more easily trust and not lose heart of faith in the midst of difficulties or even catastrophic events, because they are able to recognize these difficult or hard events as providential acts of God. These times and events may involve unpleasantness, pain, and suffering, but the yielded and guided Christian is capable of remaining Spirit-filled and able to face difficulties with trust, hope, and even joy.

No greater example exists of such a Spirit-filled person than Jesus Christ, who left the glories of heaven, to live in poverty and face opposition so He could obediently follow the Spirit's guidance, successfully become the sin-sacrifice needed by all people, and thus fulfill everything His Father wanted Him to accomplish.

DO NOT GRIEVE THE SPIRIT

While quenching the Spirit has the suddenness of a Christian deliberately choosing to ignore the Spirit's Scriptural guidance and choosing to do what they wish instead – grieving the Spirit occurs when sin has become habitual in the life of the Christian. Unyielding nonsubmission has established itself as the Christian's experience. In order to no longer grieve the Spirit, the Christian must choose to discontinue the habitual sin, so that he or she may return to the state of being filled by the Spirit again.

Habitual sin causes the Spirit grief.

We have already seen in an earlier chapter that the Holy Spirit is a Person. He is hurt or grieved when His fellowship, guidance, teaching, and power are hindered in the Christian's life. Although He remains indwelled in the Christian, the willful, continued sin prevents Him from accomplishing His work in the believer's life. There is NO loss of relationship between God and the Christian – even with habitual sin, the Christian remains a child of God because of his belief in Christ as Savior and Christ's faithful efficacy. However, the grief the believer causes by refusing to yield to the power of the Spirit and abandoning the habitual sin, causes a loss of fellowship, communication, instruction, and power from the Spirit.

The Christian may grieve the Spirit for days, months, or even years by refusing to yield to the teaching and guidance of the Spirit. During this period of rebellious willfulness, the Spirit will continue to try and reach the recalcitrant Christian with Scripture passages, advice, or counsel of family members or friends, increasingly difficult life situations, or even growing softer and less communicative and active in the person's life – oftentimes, using all these measures over time. When a Christian finally becomes aware that he or she has grieved the Spirit, the solution is to STOP whatever is causing the offense. Fortunately, Scripture promises:

> "If we confess our sins, He is faithful and righteous, so that He will forgive us our sins and cleanse us from all unrighteousness" (1 John 1:9).

The solution is to stop what is causing the Spirit grief.

The Christian's salvation and relationship with God were never lost because of the power of Christ's sacrifice, but restorative fellowship can now be re-experienced because the believer has chosen to stop grieving the Spirit with habitual sin. As it is written in the Word:

> "My little children, I am writing these things to you so that you may not sin. And if anyone sins, we have an Advocate with the Father, Jesus Christ the righteous; and He Himself is the propitiation for our sins; and not for ours only, but also for *the sins of* the whole world" (1 John 2:1-2).

This restored fellowship and relationship aren't like seeking justice in a court, but more like a hurt relationship between an erring son and a loving Father finally being healed when the son admits his wrong.

Samson grieved the Spirit and suffered the consequences.

Examples of people grieving the Spirit are found throughout the Old and New Testament. Samson had clear guidance about how to live separately and distinctively from the Philistines, but he chose to follow his own desires and preferences. He had the Spirit, family, and circumstances try to deter him, but he plunged ahead with his choices. The Spirit of God had become so diminished in his life, that during a crisis moment, Samson didn't even know the Spirit had stopped empowering him. As a result, he was completely overwhelmed and defeated by his poor choices. However, when he acknowledged his own stubborn willfulness and sin, the Spirit was able to use him for one final act.

Solomon and Demas also grieved the Spirit through sin.

Solomon knew the Scriptures better than any man of his time and had decades of the Holy Spirit giving him supernatural wisdom. When he chose to disobey clear guidance from both the Holy Spirit and the Scriptures, his life was reduced to frustration and ineffectiveness. In the New Testament, Demas was a Christian who proved his value to the Apostle Paul in his early ministry years but later become ineffective when he became worldly rather than remaining true to the Spirit and the Word. Any Christian can lose effectiveness for the cause of Christ by willfully grieving the Spirit through habitual sin.

But take heart; there is good news: God has given us the simple act of confession to bring us back into relationship and usefulness.

WALK BY THE SPIRIT

Walking by the Spirit (Galatians 5:16) is a positive command, in contrast to the two previous commands, do not quench and do not grieve the Spirit, which were negative. It is a command to take hold of the power and potential of the Holy Spirit indwelling all Christians. It is a present tense command that indicates we need to "keep on walking in the Spirit" (i.e., walking in the Spirit SHOULD be the norm for Christians and an ongoing, continual activity).

Yielding and submitting to the Spirit ensures we will produce fruit and fulfill commands of Scripture.

Walking in the Spirit is a faith-based action. It is a Christian trusting the Holy Spirit to lead, guide, empower, speak, and act through them. As we've already noted, only Christ can live the perfect Christian life. Only the Spirit of Christ can do it through us. We are His temple and earthen container. The Holy Spirit is best shown as a contrast to the human home from which He acts:

> "But we have this treasure in earthen containers, so that the extraordinary *greatness* of the power will be of God and not from ourselves" (2 Corinthians 4:7).

When we submit ourselves to His control, then and only then, can we fulfill every single command of Scripture. When we yield ourselves to Him, then and only then can the fruit of the Spirit be produced in our lives by Christ, the True Vine. When we are filled by the Spirit, then and only then can we navigate any conversation, situation, or experience with the mind of Christ – just as Jesus brilliantly and decisively handled every situation that confronted Him.

So why don't more Christians live the Spirit-filled life?

Beginning to live the Christ-filled or Spirit-filled life as a norm is difficult for several reasons:

- Christians live in a sin-filled world, currently controlled by Satan and his demons.
- Christians are soldiers for God and are always engaged in spiritual battle with evil forces and influences.
- Christians, while new creations because of Christ in them, also retain their old nature, which is becoming more and more corrupt each day. One lives moment by moment in the power of the Spirit, or in the degenerating power of their old nature.

Some Christian teachings promote an erroneous idea that maturing, Spirit-filled Christians can eventually reach a state of sinless perfection. That concept is nowhere to be found in Scripture. Instead, the constant teaching of *The Bible* is for Christians to mature (and therefore desire to sin less) by learning to appropriate the power of the Holy Spirit in their daily walk.

<u>*Living the Spirit-filled life requires making moment by moment choices.*</u>

If you think of your spiritual walk as a muscle that grows, some mature believers (no matter their age) may be spiritual body builders or triathletes, while most Christians have membership access to a divine personal trainer (the Holy Spirit). However, they constantly get tempted to stop at the world's donut shops before meeting and training with, learning from, and excelling through daily contact with the Holy Spirit.

A muscle grows when it experiences micro-trauma; little tears and breaks from exercise that then heal during sleep and rest. This regular pattern of tearing and healing results in a bigger and stronger muscle. The Spirit-filled life is like that muscle… trials, problems, and opposition the Christian faces may tear or result in micro-trauma to one's soul – but the Holy Spirit, if relied upon rather than one's own strength, resources, talents, or brains, will strengthen the Christian through rest and refreshment with Christ. This is done through studying the Word, attending church, having fellowship with other believers, and prayer with Christ, to name just a few.

When we are weary, He calls us to come to Him instead of trying harder in our own strength. He tells us His yoke is easy, and we should take it upon ourselves so we can learn to walk side by side with Him. When we walk, learn, and do ministry following His lead, we grow, mature, and successfully bear fruit.

RESULTS OF BEING FILLED WITH THE SPIRIT

The *Bible* has many things to say about the results of what happens when Christians are filled with the Spirit. Let's take a look at some of the pertinent Scriptures:

- The Christian progressively becomes more like Christ, producing the fruit of the Spirit (Galatians 5:22-23).
- The Christian is taught spiritual truth directly by the Holy Spirit (John 16:12-14).
- The Holy Spirit illumines and highlights the Scriptures so the Christian can know how to respond in every situation (Romans 8:14; 12:2).
- The Christian has assurance that his or her salvation can never be lost (Romans 8:16).
- True worship and love of God are only possible as the Christian is filled with the Spirit (Ephesians 5:18-20; John 4:24).
- The Christian's prayer life is made effective (Romans 8:26).

It's exciting to think about how much we can accomplish if we tap into the power of the Holy Spirit and start exercising our spiritual muscles to gain the strength that is freely available to us. We just need to submit and yield to Him. But in so doing, we also realize that there are many aspects to the Holy Spirit, which can lead to confusion. Join me as I address this topic in the next chapter.

Chapter Ten

WHY IS THE CHURCH CONFUSED ABOUT THE FILLING OF THE SPIRIT?

In my many years of ministry, I find that there is often much confusion about the different ministries of the Holy Spirit. Why is that? Have you experienced that confusion? Most Christians don't struggle with understanding that the Spirit **regenerates** sinners when He indwells them, transforming them into forgiven Christians. They usually grasp the concept that the Spirit **seals** Christians at the same moment He indwells them, so that they are forever owned, protected, and secured by God. However, when the Bible speaks of the **baptism** and the **filling** of the Holy Spirit, it seems that much confusion exists. Some Christians argue that the baptism and filling are two different and distinct experiences, while others argue they are synonymous. Let's look to the Scriptures to provide an answer.

The Baptism with the Spirit Occurs to All Christians; the Filling Does Not.

The Scriptures teach that the baptism with the Holy Spirit occurs at the moment of salvation and results in Christians being brought immediately into the body of Christ. In other words, all believers are baptized with the Spirit and joined to the Body of Christ (the Church) when they are saved.

> "For by one Spirit we were all baptized into one body, whether Jews or Greeks, whether slaves or free, and we were all made to drink of one Spirit" (1 Corinthians 12:13).

Baptism is a **one-time** occurrence for all Christians, just as the Holy Spirit's indwelling and sealing are also one-time occurrences.

The filling of the Holy Spirit is choosing to obey the command to be filled.

However, the filling of the Holy Spirit is something that may occur repeatedly after the person is saved. In fact, Paul commanded the Ephesians, who were believers, to be continually filled with the Holy Spirit in Ephesians 5:18. It is possible for a Christian to disobey this command and not to be filled with the Spirit, but it is impossible for a Christian not to be baptized with the Holy Spirit. Filling is choosing to obey the command to be filled; baptism, like indwelling and sealing are all acts that the Holy Spirit does on every Christian the moment they become saved. The baptism by the Holy Spirit is non-repeatable. **No one in Scripture is ever listed as receiving the baptism by the Spirit more than once. It is a one-time experience for each believer.**

In contrast, the filling of the Holy Spirit occurs many times in the lives of obedient Christians, as it did in the lives of the early apostles. The confusion sometimes arises because in the Book of Acts' account of the beginning of the Church, known as the Day of Pentecost, the apostles and their followers were indwelled, baptized with the Spirit, sealed, and filled all at the same time. That was because Pentecost was the start of what Jesus had promised to His disciples, and it was the beginning of the Church of Christ. The apostles and others were filled with the Spirit according to Acts 2:4, when they were also sealed and baptized with the Spirit. Just two chapters later, at another time and place, they were filled with the Spirit again (but NOT baptized nor sealed by the Spirit).

> "And when they had prayed, the place where they had gathered together was shaken, and they were all filled with the Holy Spirit and *began* to speak the word of God with boldness" (Acts 4:31).

It is important not to confuse baptism and filling.

Just as there are repeated instances of the filling of the disciples with the Spirit in the book of Acts, all Christians can AND SHOULD be "filled" or controlled by the Holy Spirit on many different occasions. As they mature as Christians, the practice of being filled or yielding to the Spirit as a daily, hourly, and moment-by-moment way of life should become the norm. In fact, the baptism is a separate work of the Holy Spirit and is a necessary prerequisite to place a forgiven sinner in the body of Christ, so that he or she may begin to follow the command to be filled with the Spirit. The baptism of the Holy Spirit is **an act that God does**. The filling of the Holy Spirit is a **choice the Christian makes** to obey God's command. It has to do with living a Christian life in the Spirit's power rather than one's own power.

SO... What Happened at Pentecost?

Since the baptism and the filling are two different works of the Holy Spirit, what exactly happened on the Day of Pentecost? Let's look a little deeper at that day. The confusion comes because Jesus promised the baptism of the Spirit a few days before Pentecost (Acts 1:5), and a little later, the text says that on the Day of Pentecost, the apostles were filled with the Spirit (Acts 2:4). Both occurred, as did the indwelling and sealing of the Holy Spirit – but all are separate, distinct works or ministries of the Spirit. Only the filling of the Spirit is a repeatable act.

Because the believers were baptized with the Holy Spirit, they were able to receive the Spirit's filling. Three important points should be made and emphasized:

1. The baptism with the Spirit occurs at the moment of salvation. Every believer is baptized with the Holy Spirit. However, it is possible for believers not to be filled with the Holy Spirit.

2. The baptism with the Holy Spirit occurs only once, while the filling of the Spirit may occur repeatedly throughout the Christian's lifetime.

3. Christians directly experience the filling of the Spirit and often act with boldness or manifest some other ability they would not normally have or do. For example, they may boldly share their faith, even in a public setting, although they are normally a shy or reticent personality. Another example is they may practice hospitality or service towards others, when they've never done such acts before; or they want to teach the Scriptures to others at their church when they've never taught before. It is the gifting and the filling of the Spirit that enables them to begin acting and serving in a way which is novel to them.

4. Christians do not experience the baptism with the Holy Spirit. It is an action of God, just like indwelling and sealing. Christians are never commanded to be baptized with the Holy Spirit; they are commanded to be continually filled with the Holy Spirit.

Chapter Eleven

Promises of Christ to You

If there is one person whose promises are guaranteed, it is Jesus Christ. He saved us through His dependability, trustworthiness, and sacrifice. He left heaven and accomplished the master plan designed by the Godhead in eternity past. He saved us, in spite of ourselves, and rescued us from our total helplessness. Furthermore, His promises about the Spirit and how we should be experiencing that Spirit are important for our Christian walk:

> "So, if you, *despite* being evil, know how to give good gifts to your children, **how much more will your heavenly Father give the Holy Spirit** to those who ask Him?" (Luke 11:13)

> "On the last and greatest day of the feast, Jesus stood up and called out in a loud voice, "If anyone is thirsty, let him come to Me and drink. Whoever believes in Me, as the Scripture has said**: 'Streams of living water will flow from within him.' He was speaking about the Spirit**, whom those who believed in Him were later to receive." (John 7:37-39)

> "When they arrest you and hand you over, do not worry beforehand about what you are to say, but say whatever is given you in that hour; **for it is not you who speak, but it is the Holy Spirit**." (Mark 13:11)

> "**It is the Spirit who gives life**; the flesh profits nothing; the words that I have spoken to you are spirit and are life." (John 6:63)

> "I will ask the Father, and He will give you **another Helper, that He may be with you forever;**" (John 14:16)

"But **the Helper, the Holy Spirit**, whom the Father will send in My name, **He will teach you all things, and bring to your remembrance all that I said to you.**" (John 14:26)

"When the Helper comes, whom I will send to you from the Father, that is **the Spirit of truth** who proceeds from the Father, **He will testify about Me**..." (John 15:26)

"But I tell you the truth, it is to your advantage that I go away; for if I do not go away, the Helper will not come to you; but if I go, **I will send Him to you**." (John 16:7)

"... but **you will receive power when the Holy Spirit has come upon you**; and **you shall be My witnesses** both in Jerusalem, and in all Judea and Samaria, and even to the remotest part of the earth." (Acts 1:8)

The Spirit is the source for leading the Christian life.

More promises could be listed; these just mentioned are a selection to reinforce the magnitude of Jesus's promises. The Triune God has planned since eternity past to offer Christ as the sacrifice for mankind's sin and to send the Spirit as the power source for living as a new creation. The Spirit, which God used to create the universe from nothing, now lives inside every believer to give the power needed to live a Christ-like life. The Spirit, which originated and guided the writing of Scripture, now leads and guides believers, moment by moment, with those same Scriptures. He comforts, leads, guides, teaches, convicts, and prays for us. He is the source for living the Christian life like Christ did and would have us do. He will do all this for us, if we don't keep or harbor unconfessed and unrepented sin, but instead yield to the Spirit so we can live like Jesus through the power of the Spirit in us.

What an exciting challenge! You can begin to l ve the Christ-like or Spirit-filled life today. Thus, I hope this book has answered many of your questions and concerns and revealed to you how accessible the power of the Holy Spirit is when you choose to follow Christ. If it has, my prayers for you will have been answered.

ABOUT THE AUTHOR

R. Michael Coffey (D. Min.) serves as the Executive Pastor of Burke Community Church, Burke, VA, outside of Washington D.C. He joined the staff after serving 30 years as an Army Chaplain, his last assignment was serving as the Chief of Staff, U. S. Army Chaplaincy. This role positioned him to quickly assimilate in the busy church life, first as the Pastor of Adult Ministries and currently as the Executive Pastor. Early on in his career, he also served for 5 years as a missionary with CRU. He attended Dallas Theological Seminary and later completed his Doctor of Ministry degree at Fuller Theological Seminary. Writing this book gave him the opportunity to share Scriptural truths about living the Christ-like life through trusting in God's promises, obeying the commands of Scripture, and yielding to the Holy Spirit, all of which greatly impacted his life and career. t is his prayer that those truths will impact yours as well.

Made in the USA
Middletown, DE
12 March 2023

26570609R00036